This book belongs to

_____

_____

_____

_____

The

Little Polar Bear

Birthday Book

Hans de Beer

North-South Books
New York

Hans de Beer's Little Polar Bear first appeared in the books
Little Polar Bear and *Ahoy There, Little Polar Bear*
published by North-South Books.

First published in Great Britain, Canada,
Australia and New Zealand in 1989 by North-South Books,
an imprint of Nord-Süd Verlag AG, Gossau Zürich, Switzerland
ISBN 1-55858-081-6

3 5 7 9 10 8 6 4 2

Printed in Germany

January

1 _____

_____

_____

2 _____

_____

_____

3 _____

_____

_____

4 _____

_____

_____

5 _____

_____

_____

January

6 _____

_____

_____

7 _____

_____

_____

8 _____

_____

_____

9 _____

_____

_____

10 _____

_____

_____

January

11 _____

_____

_____

January

12 _____

_____

_____

13 _____

_____

_____

14 _____

_____

_____

15 _____

_____

_____

16 _____

_____

_____

January

17 _____

_____

_____

18 _____

_____

_____

19 _____

_____

_____

20 _____

_____

_____

21 _____

_____

_____

January

22 _____

_____

_____

23 _____

_____

_____

24 _____

_____

_____

25 _____

_____

_____

26 _____

_____

_____

January

27 _____

_____

_____

28 _____

_____

_____

29 _____

_____

_____

30 _____

_____

_____

31 _____

_____

_____

January

February

1 _____

_____

_____

2 _____

_____

_____

3 _____

_____

_____

4 _____

_____

_____

5 _____

_____

_____

February

6 _____

_____

_____

7 _____

_____

_____

8 _____

_____

_____

9 _____

_____

_____

10 _____

_____

_____

February

11 _____

_____

_____

12 _____

_____

_____

13 _____

_____

_____

14 _____

_____

_____

15 _____

_____

_____

February

16 _____

_____

_____

17 _____

_____

_____

18 _____

_____

_____

19 _____

_____

_____

20 _____

_____

_____

February

21 _____

_____

_____

22 _____

_____

_____

23 _____

_____

_____

24 _____

_____

_____

25 _____

_____

_____

February

26 _____

_____

_____

27 _____

_____

_____

28 _____

_____

_____

29 _____

_____

_____

February

March

1 _____

_____

_____

2 _____

_____

_____

3 _____

_____

_____

4 _____

_____

_____

5 _____

_____

_____

March

6 _____

_____

_____

7 _____

_____

_____

8 _____

_____

_____

9 _____

_____

_____

10 _____

_____

March

11 _____

_____

_____

12 _____

_____

_____

13 _____

_____

_____

14 _____

_____

_____

15 _____

_____

_____

March

16 _____

_____

_____

March

17 _____

_____

_____

18 _____

_____

_____

19 _____

_____

_____

20 _____

_____

_____

21 _____

_____

_____

March

22 _____

_____

_____

23 _____

_____

_____

24 _____

_____

_____

25 _____

_____

_____

26 _____

_____

_____

March

27 _____

_____

_____

28 _____

_____

_____

29 _____

_____

_____

30 _____

_____

_____

31 _____

_____

_____

March

April

1 _____

_____

_____

2 _____

_____

_____

3 _____

_____

_____

4 _____

_____

_____

5 _____

_____

_____

April

6 _____

_____

_____

7 _____

_____

_____

8 _____

_____

_____

9 _____

_____

_____

10 _____

_____

_____

April

11 _____

_____

_____

12 _____

_____

_____

13 _____

_____

_____

14 _____

_____

_____

15 _____

_____

_____

April

16 _____

_____

_____

17 _____

_____

_____

18 _____

_____

_____

19 _____

_____

_____

20 _____

_____

_____

April

21 _____

_____

_____

22 _____

_____

_____

23 _____

_____

_____

24 _____

_____

_____

25 _____

_____

_____

April

26 _____

_____

_____

27 _____

_____

_____

28 _____

_____

_____

29 _____

_____

_____

30 _____

_____

_____

April

May

1 _____

_____

2 _____

_____

3 _____

_____

4 _____

_____

5 _____

_____

May

6 _____

_____

_____

7 _____

_____

_____

8 _____

_____

_____

9 _____

_____

_____

10 _____

_____

_____

May

11 _____

_____

_____

12 _____

_____

_____

13 _____

_____

_____

14 _____

_____

_____

15 _____

_____

_____

May

16 _____

_____

_____

May

17 _____

_____

_____

18 _____

_____

_____

19 _____

_____

_____

20 _____

_____

_____

21 _____

_____

_____

May

22 _____

_____

_____

23 _____

_____

_____

24 _____

_____

_____

25 _____

_____

_____

26 _____

_____

_____

May

27 _____

_____

_____

28 _____

_____

_____

29 _____

_____

_____

30 _____

_____

_____

31 _____

_____

_____

May

June

1 _____

_____

_____

2 _____

_____

_____

3 _____

_____

_____

4 _____

_____

_____

5 _____

_____

_____

June

6 _____

_____

_____

7 _____

_____

_____

8 _____

_____

_____

9 _____

_____

_____

10 _____

_____

_____

11 _____

_____

_____

12 _____

_____

_____

13 _____

_____

_____

14 _____

_____

_____

15 _____

_____

_____

June

16 _____

_____

17 _____

_____

18 _____

_____

19 _____

_____

20 _____

_____

June

21 _____

_____

_____

22 _____

_____

_____

23 _____

_____

_____

24 _____

_____

_____

25 _____

_____

_____

June

26 _____

_____

_____

27 _____

_____

_____

28 _____

_____

_____

29 _____

_____

_____

30 _____

_____

_____

June

July

1 _____

_____

2 _____

_____

3 _____

_____

4 _____

_____

5 _____

_____

July

6 _____

_____

_____

7 _____

_____

_____

8 _____

_____

_____

9 _____

_____

_____

10 _____

_____

_____

July

11 _____

_____

_____

12 _____

_____

_____

13 _____

_____

_____

14 _____

_____

_____

15 _____

_____

_____

July

16 _____

_____

_____

July

17 _____

_____

_____

18 _____

_____

_____

19 _____

_____

_____

20 _____

_____

_____

21 _____

_____

_____

July

22 _____

_____

_____

23 _____

_____

_____

24 _____

_____

_____

25 _____

_____

_____

26 _____

_____

_____

July

27 _____

_____

28 _____

_____

29 _____

_____

30 _____

_____

31 _____

_____

July

August

1 _____

_____

_____

2 _____

_____

_____

3 _____

_____

_____

4 _____

_____

_____

5 _____

_____

_____

August

6 _____

_____

_____

7 _____

_____

_____

8 _____

_____

_____

9 _____

_____

_____

10 _____

_____

_____

August

11 _____

_____

12 _____

_____

13 _____

_____

14 _____

_____

15 _____

_____

August

17 _____

_____

18 _____

_____

19 _____

_____

20 _____

_____

21 _____

_____

August

22 _____

_____

23 _____

_____

24 _____

_____

25 _____

_____

26 _____

_____

August

27 _____

_____

_____

28 _____

_____

_____

29 _____

_____

_____

30 _____

_____

_____

31 _____

_____

_____

August

September

1 _____

_____

_____

2 _____

_____

_____

3 _____

_____

_____

4 _____

_____

_____

5 _____

_____

_____

September

6 _____

_____

_____

7 _____

_____

_____

8 _____

_____

_____

9 _____

_____

_____

10 _____

_____

_____

September

11

12

13

14

15

September

16 _____

_____

17 _____

_____

18 _____

_____

19 _____

_____

20 _____

_____

September

21 _____

_____

_____

22 _____

_____

_____

23 _____

_____

_____

24 _____

_____

_____

25 _____

_____

_____

September

26 _____

_____

_____

27 _____

_____

_____

28 _____

_____

_____

29 _____

_____

_____

30 _____

_____

_____

September

October

1 _____

_____

_____

2 _____

_____

_____

3 _____

_____

_____

4 _____

_____

_____

5 _____

_____

_____

October

6 _____

_____

7 _____

_____

8 _____

_____

9 _____

_____

10 _____

_____

_____

October

11 _____

_____

_____

12 _____

_____

_____

13 _____

_____

_____

14 _____

_____

_____

15 _____

_____

_____

October

16 _____

_____

_____

October

17 _____

_____

_____

18 _____

_____

_____

19 _____

_____

_____

20 _____

_____

_____

21 _____

_____

_____

October

22 _____

_____

_____

23 _____

_____

_____

24 _____

_____

_____

25 _____

_____

_____

26 _____

_____

_____

October

27 _____

_____

_____

28 _____

_____

_____

29 _____

_____

_____

30 _____

_____

_____

31 _____

_____

_____

October

November

1 _____

_____

_____

2 _____

_____

_____

3 _____

_____

_____

4 _____

_____

_____

5 _____

_____

_____

November

6 _____

_____

_____

7 _____

_____

_____

8 _____

_____

_____

9 _____

_____

_____

10 _____

_____

_____

November

11 _____

_____

_____

12 _____

_____

_____

13 _____

_____

_____

14 _____

_____

_____

15 _____

_____

_____

November

16 _____

_____

_____

17 _____

_____

_____

18 _____

_____

_____

19 _____

_____

_____

20 _____

_____

_____

November

21

22

23

24

25

November

26 _____

_____

_____

27 _____

_____

_____

28 _____

_____

_____

29 _____

_____

_____

30 _____

_____

_____

November

December

1 _____

_____

_____

2 _____

_____

_____

3 _____

_____

_____

4 _____

_____

_____

5 _____

_____

_____

December

6 _____

_____

_____

7 _____

_____

_____

8 _____

_____

_____

9 _____

_____

_____

10 _____

_____

_____

December

11 _____

_____

_____

12 _____

_____

_____

13 _____

_____

_____

14 _____

_____

_____

15 _____

_____

_____

December

16 _____

_____

_____

December

17 _____

_____

_____

18 _____

_____

_____

19 _____

_____

_____

20 _____

_____

_____

21 _____

_____

_____

December

22 _____

_____

_____

23 _____

_____

_____

24 _____

_____

_____

25 _____

_____

_____

26 _____

_____

_____

December

27 _____

_____

_____

28 _____

_____

_____

29 _____

_____

_____

30 _____

_____

_____

31 _____

_____

_____

December

Notes

_____

_____

_____

_____

_____

_____

_____

_____

_____

_____

_____

_____

_____

_____

_____

_____

_____

_____

_____

_____